From **Frantic** to **FOCUSED**

TO DO:
Pay bills
Clean kitchen
Call vet
File receipts
Health insurance
JJ bath
Call Mom
Organize receipts
Hair appt
Soccer supplies
Return phone calls
Website updates
Article deadline
Airline tickets
Cat food
Family reunion
Thank you cards
Cancel cable
Close bank account
Schedule photographer
Organize photos
Dr. appointment
Write a will
Appreciation gifts
Farm co-op
Get a juicer
Delete emails
New phone charger
Library drop off
Charity donations
Dry cleaner
Order vitamins
Medium

How to Shift Your Life
from
Out-of-Control
to
Streamlined
and
Successful

©2017 by Beth Caldwell and PA Family Publishing

Published by PA Family Publishing

Cover Design by Daniel Szwedko Graphics
Photo by Sean Schachner

ISBN-13: 978-1541139886

ISBN-10: 1541139887

To include any part of this book as a resource in your publication, for professional training, etc., contact Beth Caldwell at (412) 202-6983 or beth@beth-caldwell.com.

Dedication

To Mom, who always encouraged me to write,
even before I could read.

Betty,

Stay Focused!

Beth Caldwell

Table of Contents

Introduction

A few years ago, while walking through a Psychic Fair, a woman grabbed my arm and said to me, "You are going to influence the world." That was odd. Since I had not asked for a prediction, she took me by surprise. I must have had a funny look on my face, because she immediately said, "I don't usually do that, but I felt like you needed to know. Whatever the story is that you want to tell, please tell it, and don't wait."

A year later, during an astrological reading I was told that in the next two years everything I'd been working on for my entire life would come to fruition. Again, I was told, "Tell your story, and don't wait."

I've been a writer and speaker for more than a decade. This is my first book that is non-business. Here, I'm sharing my personal life stories, including the obstacles and accomplishments. I hope you feel inspired, motivated and refreshed by them.

Beth

One
Meet a Frantic Lady

When this photo was taken things looked really good in my life. When I left my husband, my sons Brian, (left) was 22 months old and Kevin, (right) was only 8 weeks old. Divorce had not been in my plans. After all, no one walks down the aisle dreaming of divorce, do they?

By the time my boys reached middle school, as they are pictured here, I managed to rebuild our lives to a very respectable level. It was important to me to be present in the lives of my sons, so a 40 hour corporate job was out of the question. While working part time to support us, I became an entrepreneur on the side and created a successful business publishing a community magazine.

To the outside world, I had it all. Distinguished business owner, influence, respect, smart and athletic children, and a good-looking, successful and smart boyfriend. I participated frequently in community events, volunteered for charitable organizations, was active in my church and community and received numerous awards and recognitions for my professional accomplishments and leadership. As a single mom, I even purchased a home, without support from my dad, boyfriend or ex-husband. Things looked really good. But looks can be deceiving.

In reality, the woman in the photo was living a frantic existence. Yes, I was successful, and yes, I was happy. I was a dedicated mom raising two intelligent young men. I had accomplished a great deal at a young age. However, things weren't as polished as they appeared. I had created habits that were literally killing me.

My days were spent reacting and responding to work issues, employee mistakes and the needs of others. My evenings were spent doing housework, laundry and errands. My nights were spent working. I slept very little, ate mostly restaurant and fast food and most months had just enough to pay my bills. Looking back now, I can see that what was about to happen was inevitable. But at that time, I never could have imagined the surprise that life had in store for me.

Two
Life Turns Upside Down

During this time of my life, I used to pride myself on being "busy". I wore busy like a badge. At least one night a week, I did not go to sleep, because I was able to get the most work done when everyone else was in bed. Other nights I slept three to four hours and I never napped. I skipped meals every day and avoided going to the bathroom. I didn't want to take the time to walk all the way down the hall to the ladies room for fear of being distracted or missing an important email or phone call. I booked appointments back to back, never giving myself a break, and I said yes to every invitation, request and opportunity.

As my business grew, and the books became more popular, scheduling became even more chaotic with book signings, speaking engagements and public appearances. It wasn't uncommon for a workday to begin at 7 a.m. and end at 11 p.m.

During a particularly stressful holiday season, my boyfriend Paul and I decided to plan a weekend escape. We purchased a romantic getaway as a Christmas gift to each other and set it up for the week before Valentine's Day. I looked forward to this getaway for weeks. As single parents, we rarely got alone time and we were both looking forward to the three-day vacation.

The morning that we left, I had a tickle in my throat. The next day I had an annoying cough, but I pushed through and we enjoyed all the planned activities. When I awoke on the day that we were returning home, I felt oddly weak and dizzy. During the 3 ½ hour drive, I asked Paul to turn off the radio. The sound was hurting my ears. I slept. When we got close to home, I sat up and said to Paul, "Take me to the hospital."

I had never in my life felt so sick. I had the feeling that this was serious, very serious. Paul drove us to an Urgent Care Facility and helped me in the door. I remember the nurses complimenting me on my manicure and my shoes as I faded in and out of consciousness. After X-rays, blood and urine testing, I was diagnosed with bacterial pneumonia, a bladder infection and exhaustion. "Follow up with your primary doctor in three to five days.", the attending doctor said to me as she handed Paul several prescriptions to fill, "And rest.", she added sternly.

Three to five days, I thought. I can handle that. I'll sleep, eat chicken soup, drink herbal tea, and catch up on my favorite TV shows. I wish it had been that simple.

Three weeks went by and I was not better. Three more weeks, and I was still not able to be out of bed more than a few hours. I was too weak to drive, walk up the steps by myself, do laundry, shop, even shower without help. I had to hire a home health aid to take care of us. Friends, family and our church community helped with driving the boys to their activities, shopping and meals. A visiting nurse came once a week. I did not leave my house the entire month of March. In April, as I regained my strength, instead of slowly getting back to work, I jumped right in, worked a full week and had a relapse. I found myself feeling even weaker than before and spent another three weeks in bed. I had taken on a lot of challenges in life and I was used to winning. Pneumonia was the toughest adversary I'd ever faced, and I was losing.

For the first time in my life it occurred to me that I might not get better and I began to panic. My sons were too young to take care of themselves. The possibility of being a young sick woman had never entered my mind. Worry and panic became my new companions. I began to ask my church-going friends for prayers and asked for the elders of a local church to come and give me a blessing. I asked my non-traditional, metaphysical and holistic friends for healing energy and potions. A lot of people were praying for me to get better and it wasn't happening. At least not fast enough for me.

My physical break-down was quickly turning into an emotional crisis. I remember one difficult afternoon where I googled my symptoms and discovered for the first time in my life that I was experiencing anxiety. "How can this be happening?", I scolded myself, "Why are you so weak? What has happened to you?"

The next day I received a get-well card from a colleague. It included a kind note, a grocery store gift card and this message:

"Sometimes things have to fall apart so that better things can come together"
--Marilyn Monroe

"What does that mean?", I asked myself. That quote really touched me. I hung it on the refrigerator thoughtfully, then went back and took it down. I sat with the quote in my hands and thought about this. It had never occurred to me that my life needed to change. I remembered some advice that had been given to me, something that I brushed off at the time. Someone told me that God sends us messages and life lessons with experiences. If we don't learn our lesson from the first experience we get another experience. Our experiences will continue and become more serious until we learn the what we're meant to learn. Eventually, we have to listen or we'll die never having learned.

Finally, I said aloud, "What am I supposed to be learning here? What am I not seeing?"
"God", I demanded, "Are you trying to tell me something?"
God smiled. Starting that day, things got better.

Three
The Transition Begins

The next morning I awoke feeling stronger than I had in months. I made my way from the bed to the couch. Instead of turning on the TV or computer, I lit a candle and snuggled in with my journal and a warm blanket.

"Ok, God. I'm ready. Tell me what I need to change." The messages that I received through prayer and journaling over the next few weeks changed my entire life. Through thought and introspection I realized that I had accomplished exactly the opposite of what I yearned for when starting my business. I wanted freedom and flexibility. I wanted to be paid well and have complete mastery over my schedule. What I created was exactly the opposite. I worked more hours than anyone I knew. I attended my son's sporting events, but was not fully present. I was often on the phone or using my laptop on the bleachers. I had not attended an extended family gathering in several years. Instead of owning a business, my business owned me. During these quiet hours I realized that my sickness was a direct result of poor habits and poor decisions. It took a while to get the message, but finally, I heard it loud and clear. It was time for change.

Due to my lengthy illness, I had a clear calendar, so I was able to get back to work with some new policies. For the next several months I created and nurtured new habits. Something very interesting happened. My business began to skyrocket. My life began to simplify. I finally enjoyed freedom, flexibility and profits all at the same time. And it continued to get better. I had worked hard for more than a decade, sacrificing time with family, quality of life, and my health only making just enough money to pay the bills. Now I was working less hours, making more money and truly enjoying my life. I was no longer scattered and overwhelmed. I had gone from frantic to focused. I had finally learned the lesson and realized that my life's work might be much more than I imagined.

Now, I'd like to share with you the new habits that I created and embraced in hopes that you might also become a formerly frantic lady. Read on, your new start is ahead.

**New Habit
Number One:**

Stop Doing
and
Start Being

Four
Who Are You Being?

A few months before my illness, I hosted a women's conference in my home town. The purpose of the conference was to promote my soon-to-be released business book. I arranged for four dynamic speakers to present, secured the venue, solicited sponsors, vendors and volunteers, chose a lovely menu, put up a website, made flyers, created a marketing plan, sold tickets, promoted the speakers, trained the speakers to promote the event. I designed the program, collected handouts from all of the speakers and got them professionally printed. I printed all the name tags and the registration sheet on my printer at home. The day of the event, I arrived early to oversee the setup of the room, audio visual equipment and vendors and train the volunteers. The venue that I chose had a breathtaking and inspirational view. The turnout was amazing. I had created an event to be proud of.

After a carefully planned health-conscious but tasty breakfast, I welcomed the guests and announced the agenda. I was the first of four speakers. Our theme was "abundance" and my presentation was called Get Paid What You're Worth.

I remember looking out into the audience and seeing the women hang on my every word. The audience was full of smiling faces, head nodding and note-taking. This was starting out to be a fantastic event.

After my presentation, I introduced the next speaker and made my way to the back of the room to take photos. Standing in the back of the room watching her speak was just as exciting as being in the front row, everyone was listening intently. This woman was talking about attracting abundance, and she knew what she was talking about. In less than three years she had grown a coaching business for women and was enjoying a thriving practice. The women were taken with her content. The speaker was standing in front of the window and there was a stunning view of the city behind her. The sun was bright and the sky was deep blue.

One of the volunteers assisted me as I put two chairs together and climbed up on them to get a great photo. The volunteer held the chairs securely and I kicked off my shoes, climbed up and began snapping photos. I stood there taking it all in, proud of my accomplishments. At that moment, the speaker said to the audience, "One of the first questions I ask my clients is this: Who are you being? Are you the woman that you always wanted to become or are you a woman who is doing everything for everyone instead of being who you're meant to be?" The question stunned me. As I stood there, in a somewhat undignified and certainly unsafe position, I realized that I was doing lots and lots of things but I was not close to being who I wanted to be. I was flabbergasted by her comments. Since my tote bag and all of my personal belongings were in the front of the room, I dashed out into the hallway to look for paper to write on. I did not want to forget this new concept. Finding no paper, I got a napkin from one of the servers and a pen from a friendly vendor and I wrote what I had just learned on the napkin:

Stop Doing
and
Start Being

I still have that napkin today. It's one of the most important lessons learned so far in my life. I remember very little about the rest of the day, except that the coach who inspired me sold several thousand dollars in coaching packages and I sold nothing. I did put on an event to be proud of, but during all the preparation and all of my "doing", I forgot the reason that I was hosting the event to begin with. Instead of creating momentum for my upcoming book, I created a beautiful event that made a lot of money for someone else. That was a lesson that I learned the first time.

Since then I've asked myself several times, "Beth, who are you being?" It's created a transformational shift in my life and business. When I would catch myself saying "yes" to something that I didn't really want to do, I'd pause and say, "Is this who you want to be?"

The "Stop Doing and Start Being" concept has also radically influenced the way I set goals in my life. For as long as I can remember, I burdened myself with stretch goals. The kind of goals that are very ambitious but not usually realistic. I told myself that even if I didn't meet the goal, I would certainly achieve a great deal by setting it. And I always accomplished a great deal. The big problem was that I focused on my misses instead of my wins, so I was always disappointed with my progress.

After several months of living with "Stop Doing and Start

Being", I discovered that I did not want to be a woman who is striving to succeed all the time. I did not want to be frantic any more. The December after my illness, my coach asked me to pick just one word to embrace for the new year. No goals, just one way of being. This was radically different than what I was used to doing. It took me several days to select a word. I agonized over this choice. An entire year is a long time! After a morning of quiet time, I realized what my theme would be for the year. Release. I needed to release some of the commitments, projects and people that I had aligned myself with. As I discussed this with my coach, I worried, "How will I know what to release, Kim?" We decided that this was going to be a very special year for me, so she made an exception. I could have two words. That year my words were:

Clarity

and

Release

Clarity so that I would know what projects, people and commitments to agree to and which ones to let go.

Release so that I would not struggle to hang on to these agreements and situations that weren't in my best interest.

I had never before been so enthusiastic about embracing change. I created a beautiful image of my words, printed it and hung it on my bedroom mirror so that this was the first thing I saw every day. I put the words into my digital calendar on repeat so that they popped up every day at 8 a.m. and 8 p.m. This reminded me often to release what I did not need. every time I was invited to do something I reflected, "Does this

align with my life and business goals and where I'm going?"
I said yes only if I had complete clarity that it was a good fit.
Eventually, I stopped feeling guilty about saying no.

As the year went on, I began to release projects,
commitments, clients and habits that no longer served me.
I began to get a very clear picture of where I wanted my life
to go. Remember my illness from the prior year? I had an
especially clear picture of where I never wanted to go again.
At the end of that year, I had complete clarity. I wanted to be a
full time writer.

That was a scary but exciting decision. Nonetheless, I was
determined and fully committed. Within a week, after telling
no one but my immediate family, I got a call from my local
business journal offering me a column. Within six months, I
had a magazine column. And there was no looking back.

New Habit Number Two:

Implement
New
Habits

Five
New Daily Habits

After spending a lifetime and a career living in personal chaos, it was a little tricky to stop doing and start being. Not only was I accustomed to being frantically busy, I had trained everyone that I would do their work for them. Making the decision to change was the first step. Implementing my new habits and convincing others that this was a good idea required some finesse.

I knew from past failures that it was important for me to only add one new habit at a time. So I began with "Clarity" and "Release". Obviously the first thing I needed to get a handle on was my habit of overbooking myself. I had to take a good look at my commitments and decide which ones to release. Today, I can make a decision about whether an opportunity is a good fit for me in a matter of moments. Back then, I agonized over a lot of these choices because I didn't want to disappoint anyone or leave any projects unfinished.

Saying "no" after years of saying "yes" was not easy for me. At first I apologized and stammered, and felt very uncomfortable. Having a coach helped, but by this time in my life I had a strong desire for change and that made a big difference.

To keep me focused on my new way of being, I wrote the

words "Clarity" and "Release" in several places. I had note cards on my bedroom mirror, my refrigerator, the sun visor of my car, in my journal, on my desk, on the screen of my computer and the door of my office.

Because I had been very ill, most people were not surprised when I let go of projects. Fortunately, I received mostly support and encouragement from my family, friends and colleagues.

My changes did make some people uncomfortable. I received a few snide comments, "Oh, you have an ASSISTANT taking your calls, I guess you are a big shot now."
I was also subjected to manipulative behavior, "Well, Beth, if YOU don't run this fundraiser again it will surely fail. And we'll raise no money for the charity. And Beth, that would be a horrible thing. This is something you could do in your sleep, so it's really unfair to the charity for you to NOT do this project."
I even experienced some tears, "PLEASE, we can't survive here if you don't keep us as a client. We NEED you, we depend on you."

I have to admit, some things were easier to release than others. Remember that if you have trained people to depend on you, it will take them a while to get used to your new habits. Here's what worked for me:

- Staying focused on my intentions
- Reminding myself daily of my new habits
- Being pleasant but firm with my "no's"
- Reassuring others that my new habits were best for me
- Encouraging others to seek new volunteers or solutions to their issues
- Implementing only one new habit at a time

When I work with women who want to make changes, they always encounter two stumbling blocks:

1. Their own mindset.
2. The discomfort of their family, friends and colleagues.

Remember that when you want to make changes in your life, you're often addressing habits that you've had for many years. You've spent a long time nurturing them. Building better habits will take some practice. Be consistent and have a support plan to keep you motivated.

When it comes to your family, friends and colleagues, you'll need some finesse. Your changes may not fit their personal intentions. Perhaps you've taken responsibility for a colleague's work, and now you don't want to anymore. The colleague may be very uncomfortable with this new situation, and may feel cranky about it. Many people would handle the situation this way:

"Susie, I'm afraid that I can't continue to do the retail report for you anymore. My own reports are late and I'm having to work extra hours. This is really your responsibility and you are taking advantage of me by having me do your work. Will you start doing it again?"

Then Susie feels criticized, attacked and you have asked her a yes or no question with no wins for her. Even if she did say yes to this question, she will likely have a poor attitude and resent the situation.

A better way to handle this is like this:

"Susie, I was doing some long-term planning and I realized that I've been handling the retail report for the past few years and that is really your responsibility. I owe you an apology for taking that over. I should have trusted you to handle it, and made sure you had the necessary training. As a result, you've missed out on the credit and my own reports have been late. I'd like to resolve this, and I'd like you to start getting credit for the work. I think it makes sense for you to take control of this project again. I know you'll need some time to refresh yourself on the procedures, and I can arrange for you to be re-trained in the process. What month do you think you can take this back, will June or July be better for you?"

You want to carefully plan out what you're going to say and how you're going to say it. No one is going to volunteer to do work that they haven't had to do for years, especially without an increase in salary. You must show the win for them. Remember your question needs to be worded in a way that allows for the best answer for you, so think carefully about the wording of your request.

Maybe you are still doing your adult child's laundry or meal preparation. It's not fair to say, "Guess what, Johnny. I've been cooking and cleaning and doing your laundry for 33 years, and I'm done. You're on your own now." It's understandable that you might feel that way, but Johnny probably has no self-care skills at this point. You don't want Johnny to starve, wear dirty clothes, feel inadequate and resent you. Here is a better way to handle a situation like this:

"Kids, I have great news. I'm going to begin _____." (enter your plan here)
"Here's what's great about this: _____" (enter benefits here)
"You'll have to change, though" (apologize if appropriate)
"This is good for everyone because _____." (enter the wins for everyone here)

Here is a fun example:

"Kids, I have great news. I'm going to begin to take flying lessons." (pause for the shock to be absorbed) "And I realized something when I registered for my classes yesterday. By taking care of 100% of your needs all of these years, I have robbed you of important life skills, and your independence. Even though I enjoy cooking for you, it's important that you learn to cook. I apologize for not doing better with this. I'd like to start teaching you. My first lesson is on the 25th of the month. Would you like to get started on Saturday? This is going to be fun. Not only will you be able to help cook for the family, by this time next year, I'll be able to fly us all to the beach."

When you're making changes for you and you need to get them on-board, always include what's in it for them! Remember, whatever you are doing is likely a surprise to them, and was probably not in their plans, so give them time to adjust. Also, you had some time to prepare for this conversation and they haven't. If they don't respond the way you expect them to, don't be disappointed. Be patient and remember that long time habits take a while to change.

Over the next few years, I implemented even more daily habits. As I began to release commitments, I had more time and space to take care of myself. I was able to integrate important self-care routines and set up new rituals for mornings, evenings and weekends. Since then, I've had different themes for my year. Here are some of them:

Clarity

Release

Leverage

Potential

Abundance

Ascend

New habits are powerful. What's possible for you?

**New Habit
Number Three:**

Create an
Ideal Schedule

Six
The Ideal Schedule for You

During my frantic life, one of the biggest challenges that I had was an out-of-control calendar. I learned that I actually suffer from a known condition. A disorder, if you will, that is very common to people-pleasers and over-achievers. I suffer from a condition known as Time Optimism.

Time Optimism is a dangerous condition. If you don't control your calendar, your calendar will control you. Do you suffer from time optimism? It's fairly common among women today.

Here are the symptoms:

- Scheduling more things in your day than are realistically possible for any human to complete.
- Underestimating the time that it will take to complete a project or task.
- Expecting yourself to be able to do more than others.
- Taking on more responsibilities than you can handle.
- Not finishing your committed tasks on time.
- Frequently skipping meals or working late to get caught up.
- Arriving late because you failed to leave on time.
- Having to multi-task in order to get everything done.
- Having more things on your "I didn't get to it yet" list than on your "completed" list

Like any serious condition caused by bad habits, there is hope! Admitting that you are a time optimist is the first step.

I want you to tackle your to-do list first. Is it pages long? Does it have items that can be completed by someone other than you? Is it unrealistic? Would you give it to anyone else and expect them to complete those tasks in a day, a week, or even a month?

I know that your list is full of important things. Some of them are more urgent than others, so let's re-arrange those tasks in order of importance. What needs to be done this week? Start a new list with only these items and move the other tasks into your (or someone else's) calendar for next week, next month, etc. Most importantly, when you're adding tasks from your to-do list right into your calendar, you may find that you don't have time to do them for a while. This will help you to be realistic when taking on new projects, causes and tasks. Get into the new habit of carefully considering each task that you add to your to-do list. Be realistic about each completion date, otherwise you'll experience calendar chaos.

When I shared my calendar overwhelm several years ago in my women's mastermind group, I got some great advice from members, Lynda and Laura. Lynda encouraged me to block time off in my calendar between appointments for transitioning. She suggested that I allow time to complete work from the first appointment before beginning something new. This suggestion was so simple that I was embarrassed that I hadn't thought of it before. It made a lot of sense. Still, I was not sure that I could do this. I had created the habits of letting people schedule with me according to their schedules and not mine. I had taught people that I would accomodate them, and had been so flexible that I often took phone calls and meetings during the weekends, evenings, and even during family events. Laura, another member of our mastermind, said, while you are setting up this new calendar system, I suggest that you block off a half day a week where you don't have any commitments. That will allow you time to finish work that you are behind on, and you won't have to work during the evenings or weekends.

I must admit, I felt very nervous about trying this new system. After years of being flexible and accommodating, this seemed arrogant to me. Still, I had to make some changes. I was literally killing myself with exhaustion and frustration. Lynda and Laura encouraged me. They reminded me that other professionals have restricted availability. "You don't just call a dentist or a doctor or a massage therapist, or your hairdresser and get any time you want with them. They tell you their availability and you accommodate to their schedule. That's the way it works.

I resisted for a while, but the more I thought about it, the more I could see how this would be better for me. So I did it. I blocked off Friday mornings in my schedule to do administrative work and catch up. And, whenever I scheduled a one-hour appointment with someone, I blocked off two hours in my calendar to complete whatever needed done after that meeting. Something interesting began to happen. When people realized that I was not always available, they stopped asking for free time. No one ever cancelled, showed up late, or postponed an appointment because they respected my time. Within a few months I was working less hours and making more money than I had since my business began. Even more important, I wasn't exhausted. I wish I had learned this simple strategy much sooner in my life. Sometimes I get requests to work when I'm not available. If I accommodate that request, I block off an equivalent number of hours to keep from being over-booked. Remember, I'm a time-optimist, so I have a tendency to take on too much. When I see too much on my calendar, I enter a brief "NO-ZONE" period, where I say no to everything until I'm caught up.

After a few months of using this new calendar system, I started blocking off days where I could work on projects that had been neglected. This really helped me to make significant progress on several writing projects and my Leadership Academy for Women.

Can calendar blocking change your life? I bet it can. I give you permission to put calendar-blocking on your to-do list right now.

New Habit
Number Four:

Acknowledge
Your
Achievements

Seven
Acknowledge Your Achievements Not Your Shortcomings

I used to work until the wee hours of the morning. Frequently I found myself at the dining room table, a dog curled up at my feet and a cat on each side of my computer. Most of the time I'd stop around midnight or one a.m., but once or twice a week, I'd work until two a.m. or later. I would sit at the computer for hours without getting up. When I'd finally stop working, I'd shut off the computer, which was a sign to the animals that it was time for bed. The four of us would head up the stairs together.

I had an odd ritual back then. I'd start up the steps and at about step number three, I'd remember something that I'd forgotten. As I placed my tired foot on the stairs I'd say to myself, "Oh, darn! You forgot to send that email." That would remind me of something else that had been neglected. "Oh, no! You didn't sign that contract yet. It was due yesterday." "Wait, did you get the clothes out of the dryer? NO! WAIT, did you put the clothes INTO the dryer?"

With every step up the stairs, I'd remember something I didn't do. Sometimes, I'd be almost to the top and I'd turn around and go back down to do just one more thing, with the animals following. They would sigh, look at me sadly, and settle back into their positions at my side and feet. On nights that I did continue up to bed, the animals would re-settle at the foot of my bed or with the boys while my odd ritual continued. I'd lay in bed silently checking off the things that I didn't do, scolding and silently willing myself to remember to do these items as soon as I awoke. Then, I'd either lay there criticizing myself, get up and write a list, or go back downstairs to do a few more things since I wasn't able to fall asleep.

About once a month, I'd physically crash and go to bed at 10 p.m., catching up on my rest. One day, after a "crash night", I was at my local coffee shop and the waitress there exclaimed, "WOW! You look incredible." I laughed, accepting her compliment and replied, "HA! Maybe I should sleep every night." No one else laughed. They all looked at me, very perplexed. I said, "What, none of you stay up all night to get your work done?" An awkward and uncomfortable silence followed.

When I told Paul what happened in the coffee shop later that evening, he shared his own frustration about my late-night work sessions and my beating-myself-up rituals. "You know what, Beth, I wish that just once, just one time, you'd focus on what you have accomplished and stop talking about what you didn't do." At first, I was defensive. But I could see that he was sincerely upset and he looked worried about me. I tried to shake off his concerns, channeling my inner Wonder Woman. However, his reaction and the attitude of the strangers in the coffee shop troubled me. SInce I had a full night sleep the night before, I settled in at the dining room table at 10 p.m., ready for a marathon night of work. At about 1 a.m., Paul's words replayed in my head. I decided to shut down the computer and head upstairs. The animals and I made our way to the stairs and my nightly ritual began. This time, however,

I made a change. The moment that a nagging reminder came into my head, I replaced it with an accomplishment. This felt so unusual that I paused on the steps. The animals instinctively turned around and headed back downstairs, but I continued up, slowly. On each step I mentally checked off one thing that I had accomplished. At the top of the stairs, I was smiling, and felt content. I fell asleep instantly, without worry. The next morning I woke up feeling happy, not dreadful. For a long time, I continued that ritual of checking off my accomplishments on each step, and found myself feeling more confident, proud and satisfied with my work during the day. I stopped criticizing myself and I no longer worried in bed. I don't know why or how I started my negative nighttime routine, but I'm grateful that I stopped.

Today, when I overhear women criticizing themselves or agonizing over what they haven't done, I interrupt them, and say, "Can you stop for a moment right now, and make a list of what you DID get done today?" This always throws them a little, especially when they are a total stranger, say, in line at the bank, but I insist.

Look girlfriends, life is too short for you to lose sleep or worry about what you didn't get done. Please focus on your accomplishments, and when you do, you'll not only sleep better, you'll experience more joy. Teach the women around you to do the same.

**New Habit
Number Five:**

Be Careful About
Taking Advice

Eight
Be Careful Who You Listen To

Whenever you step up and do important work in the world, it will attract a lot of attention. While many people will be thrilled about what you're doing, count on the fact that you'll also make some folks uncomfortable.

As a chronic people-pleaser, I've found myself bouncing around sometimes, making changes and accommodations to suit others, and listening to the advice of every person who says to me, "Hey Beth, do you know what you should do?"

One particular memory stands out to me. I decided to create a 5-week teleclass workshop on getting publicity for your business. My idea was to record the workshop and sell it. The class was going along very well, and after the end of the second session, one of the students called me on the phone. "Beth, I don't appreciate that I have to wait to the end of the class to ask questions. I think you should offer some interaction." Wanting to please, I agreed, and so during class three, I took a break and allowed questions at the midpoint. It was a DISASTER. Many people spoke up and asked questions that were not relevant to the topic of the day. There was a little whining and worrying and the woman who wanted the time and space to interact? She didn't show up for that class. At the end of the evening, I was exhausted. The recording was not something that could be used in a package to resell, and I spent the rest of the evening criticizing myself and feeling frustrated. The next day I heard Oprah Winfrey on the radio telling a story about how she planned her talk show in a certain format. During a taping, someone in the audience suggested she do it differently, so she did. Months later, she said out loud, "How did this get so far off track?" She realized that she took someone's advice and forgot her intentions. I smiled and felt encouraged. If it took Oprah months to realize this and I discovered my mistake within one day, I was going to be just fine.

From now on, when you are uncertain of how to do something or you find yourself facing a tough decision, remember to only seek advice from those you respect and admire.

Do you want to be in a happy relationship?
Don't ask for romantic advice from your friend who hates her husband.

Do you want a successful career?
Get mentoring from someone who is content with their career and has achieved the types of goals that excite you.

Do you want to be an artist?
Get your advice from someone creative.

Do you want to take a risk and make a change?
Don't ask for advice from your friends who hate change.

Most of all friends, I want you to stop trying to please others. Make your decisions based on your own internal guidance system. I'd rather you not ask advice from anyone. Instead, spend time alone, quietly reflecting and listening to the messages of your soul. Your inner guidance will never lead you down the wrong path.

When Paul and I first began dating, we'd often have to endure the question, "When are you getting married?" or "Why aren't you married?" This used to make me very uncomfortable and defensive. For some reason, many of the women in our culture feel that being married makes you legitimate. I remember one day when I was complaining about this and Paul said to me, "Beth, have you ever noticed that the people who torment you about not being married are the ones who are unhappily married?" As usual, when Paul says something profound like this, I'm speechless. He continued, "I think that the people who are miserable want you to be more like them so that they can feel legitimate."

I had to think about that for a while and really listen to that message. I never let people upset me with their questions again. And, as I started spending more of my time with high-achievers, I got that question much less frequently.

So, how should you deal with advice that is not right for you? Simply have a polite prepared response. Here are some ideas:

Thanks for that suggestion. I've never considered that.

That is a different perspective and something to consider.

That's an interesting idea. I don't think it's right for this project, but I appreciate your input.

Wow, you have certainly given this a lot of thought. I'll have to consider your suggestions and see if they make sense for what I have in mind. Thank you.

No wedding date set in the near future, but you'll be the first one to know.

Most people don't offer advice to hurt you. Many times, they genuinely want you to succeed and be happy. Appreciate their input but don't rush to make any big changes. Only take advice from someone you'd trade places with in life, or better yet, rely on your own wisdom.

**New Habit
Number Six:**

One Thought
at a Time

Nine
Slow Down Your Multi-Tasking Mind

If you've ever met me in person, listened to one of my recorded workshops, or attended one of my in-person seminars, you already know that I am a woman who talks, moves and thinks very quickly. For most of my life I believed that multitasking was my super-power. It's unexpected to have someone like me promote mindfulness.

If you're not familiar with the concept of mindfulness, it's the art of slowing your thoughts, paying attention to your thoughts and becoming intentional about what you're thinking, what you're doing and how you are behaving.

Most women have many thoughts buzzing around our brains all at once. Have you ever asked a man, "What are you thinking about?" and he replies, "Nothing."? I remember asking Paul that once and when he answered "nothing", I didn't believe him. I said, "No, really, what are you thinking?" He paused, searched his brain and said, "ummm.....nothing." I didn't believe him. Around the same time, my teenage sons were reaching adulthood. I remember being frustrated about the messy house and no one but me noticing dirty clothes on the floor or over-filled trash cans. I've never agreed with the thoughts common among my peers and colleagues that men are lazy or that they are incapable of seeing things on the floor. I knew that the men in my home were intelligent, kind and considerate people. There had to be something about this that I did not understand.

One afternoon, while getting ready to go on a trip, I was in my super-frenzy mode of packing and getting everyone organized to go away. I washed many loads of laundry in preparation, to make sure that we had all the right clothes to take along and plenty of clean clothes in the closet when we returned. I planned ahead for every possible contingency and packed accordingly. I had a bag specifically for shoes, one for books to read in the car, one for activities for the family while we were away, selected several coats and jackets to be ready for any weather possibility and a garment bag for myself with dress and casual clothes since this was a combined business trip and family vacation. Paul was going to join us after work and I wanted to be ready to go when he arrived, so I was barking orders at Brian and Kevin. "OK, let's put these bags in the trunk, and these bags in the back seat, and OH GEEZ PILLOWS, EVERYONE GRAB A PILLOW, and Brian, please check JJ's food bowl and litter box, be sure that I have those ready." Brian stopped me. "MOM", he threw his hands up to his head, "Please, one thing at a time."

That stopped me. I did not think that what I was demanding of Brian was unreasonable. It seemed sensible to me to do six things at one time. It was obvious in that moment that my son could not. He simply could not. Trying to keep up with my pace was frustrating him. I slowed down slightly, doing four things myself and asking each of the boys to do one task each. Later, when I shared the experience with Paul, he said to me, "Beth, it's like I always tell you, if you would do just one thing at a time you would get a lot more done." I rolled my eyes, annoyed. It's true, he had told me this several times. And, there were several times that I suggested to him over the years, "You know you can take the trash bag down the steps at the same time that you carry the dirty clothes down." No, Paul does not multitask. His usual reply is, "I'd rather take more time and do it right than make a mistake and have to begin again."

The next time I was working at my desk, I thought, "OK, I'm going to give this a try. I'll write this article and work on only this article. How hard can it be?" Friends, this was much harder than I expected. After writing a few lines of my article, I found myself tempted to read email, view social media, pick up my cell phone to look for a text message, check on the cat, get a drink. That was just during the first minute. "I can do this.", I assured myself. A few more minutes of writing and I thought of some tasks to do for clients, an idea for a press release, wondered if I remembered to take the meat out of the freezer, wondered if it was time to get the clothes out of the dryer, and was again tempted to check email. I was tempted to give it up. "How can Paul live like this?" I wondered out loud. I am sure he has had the same thoughts about my busy brain many times.

Writing that article while doing nothing else was a struggle for me. I was determined, though, to give this "one thing at a time" routine a fair shake.

Over the next several months I tried quieting my brain several times. It took a lot of practice, and eventually I admitted that when there were less thoughts in my mind, my brain worked better. My writing seemed more focused. I felt less cluttered about my workshops and events and I stopped being stressed about getting everything done. My friends and clients noticed that I seemed less frantic. I learned about resources like Calm.com, and Mindful magazine. I tried a few meditations on YouTube. I even attended a Sunday retreat to learn meditation. My ten year old niece, Mia was shocked to learn that I was doing this. "Aunt Beth", she said, "you know that you're not allowed to talk at those things, right? Are you going to be ok?" I was fine. It was odd to be still and silent for three hours, but it was also very peaceful. The instructors took us through some group exercises, breathing exercises, and guided meditations. I found it peaceful and refreshing.

If you are afraid of giving up multitasking, you don't have to. Multitasking can still be your super power. Save it for the times when you actually need a super power instead of all day every day.

Before you get frantic about embracing mindfulness, let me tell you some things that you don't need to do.

To begin practicing meditation and mindfulness, <u>you do not need</u>:

- a designated meditation room
- special clothing
- to learn any rituals
- certifications
- to climb a mountain or go to the beach
- a gong
- a yogi
- to change your religion
- yoga lessons
- Incense
- an hourglass or timer
- a computer program, app or guide
- to sit in any special positions
- to lose weight

- to be vegan or eat a certain diet
- anyone's permission or approval

When asked to explain mindfulness during a media interview, the Dalai Lama answered, "It's a habit of daily introspection." Notice that he did not give a long and detailed description. This is a simple process of quieting your mind. For many women, having a quiet mind can be awkward, and uncomfortable. We're used to lots and lots of things going through our brains all at the same time. This is understandable because mindfulness practices are the exact opposite of what we've been conditioned to do in our lives and business. We have become goal oriented and competitive, especially with ourselves. I don't recommend that you incorporate mindfulness in this way. Many women attempt to jump on the mindfulness train like this: I'm going to become zen. I'm going to buy a special outfit, download some special music, get some incense, set up a special space in my home, buy a new journal and a pretty pen, and beginning Monday, I'll meditate every day for 30 minutes. If you're a busy woman with a busy mind, that is not going to work for you. Recognize this and don't try and force yourself to be an expert immediately.

Here is a better way to begin: put a reminder on your calendar to quiet your mind every day. It can be once a day to begin with, or try it two or three times a day. Begin by practicing for just one minute. For one minute set your intention to quiet your mind, slow your breathing and relax your entire body. It's going to feel awkward at first, and your brain will probably immediately begin to generate ideas and distractions. This is normal. Notice the thoughts and say to yourself, "I will think about that in a minute, right now I'm quieting my mind." You don't have to have a visual aid or music but you can try that, especially if it helps to quiet the distractions.

There are many benefits that can be experienced from practicing mindfulness. Some of the one's that have been especially important to me include:

- Fewer judgemental thoughts
- Trusting myself and my intuition
- Accepting myself
- Patience
- Less of a need to control situations and outcomes
- Noticing habits that are not ideal
- New awareness of things and people around me
- Appreciation of the efforts and challenges of others
- Recognizing how truly blessed I am

Some of the world's most influential people and the most innovative and successful companies incorporate mindfulness into lives and schedules every day. Adding mindfulness has been transformational for me, so I hope you'll give it a try.

**New Habit
Number Seven:**

Let Them
Solve Problems
for Themselves

Ten
Stop Solving Other People's Problems

Women are natural nurturers. We don't like to see others suffering or struggling. We like to help whenever we can. When I worked for a social service agency, I often took on the causes of my co-workers clients. I'm a very resourceful woman, with a lot of enthusiasm and high energy level. My coworkers would let their case files build up. I never saw a file as a piece of paper, I viewed each file as a family. It was common for me to stay at work late, come in on my days off, and take work home with me so that all of the clients being served by the agency were taken care of. Instead of supporting my co-workers by suggesting solutions or offering resources, I simply took over their case files. I didn't get paid extra and they didn't get paid less. When I became exhausted, I reminded myself that people were counting on me. These families had a lot bigger problems than being tired. Eventually, I became burned out. I resented my coworkers because I was doing their work and mine. They didn't mind at all. They never asked for my help.

When women take on the responsibilities of others, we keep them from learning how to do things for themselves. We think we're being kind, but we're actually hurting ourselves, and them.

Today, when I go to work with a company that it is in a crisis, inevitably I find HER. The woman who is running the organization, and usually running it into the ground. She's not the owner, the president or even an executive. She is often an admin or office manager, and she's the one person that everyone in the company goes to for everything. Let's call her Rosie.

Having an IT problem? Call Rosie. She schedules all technology repair.
Need an ID badge? Call Rosie. She arranges for all badges to be printed.
Ordering office supplies? All orders go through Rosie. Just tell her what you need.
Want to change your voice message? Rosie handles that.
Found a problem with our website? Rosie deals with the web designer.
Received an invoice? Rosie pays all the bills.
The media is calling? You better send that call to Rosie.
Upset about something? Have an idea? Do you know something that could improve our business? Please, don't mention that to Rosie. She's very sensitive and gets offended easily. Trust me, you don't want to get on her bad side.

Rosie has positioned herself as invaluable to the company. She comes in early, stays late and rarely takes vacation. She feels confident that the company will fall apart if she would take off more than a day or two. She has trained the staff to depend on her for everything. She knows every process, every system, every secret, every answer and solves every problem. Senior management treats her with kid gloves because they are paying her very little money to handle several jobs. They don't want to irritate her because they know that if she gets upset she'll cause big problems. When a talented and innovative new employee comes on board, Rosie gets territorial. Usually the new person learns very quickly to keep their head down, do a minimal amount of work, and stay out of Rosie's way. High achievers quit within a few months and move on to work with a progressive company. This always makes Rosie feel relieved.

Companies that allow a Rosie to run the business usually don't enjoy massive growth, explosive profits or receive recognition for being innovative. They stay small and don't make any changes. They call in someone like me when sales are suffering or when so many people have quit that they cannot meet their sales demands. This level of dysfunction hurts everyone. I find myself in a room with six or eight executives and I'll tell them, "You're going to have to make changes." Sometimes they would rather go out of business or close down a department than confront someone like Rosie.

Rosie's need to be needed has caused the company to lose profits. What happens when Rosie eventually gets sick, takes vacation or retires? The company has a group of employees that don't know how to do their job because someone else has been doing it for years. When the company begins to expect results, the employee becomes resentful for having to work harder for the same amount of pay.

But wait, Rosie didn't intend to cause harm, losses or disfunction, did she? No, she was being nice. Working hard. Giving extra effort. Being kind. And over the years, Rosie was never offered a raise or given a promotion. The company didn't need to, she was already doing all the work for low pay.

She already assumed the roles of higher positions without the title.

Moms do the same things when they finish homework, complete difficult tasks or fail to teach their children how to become independent. They don't do these things with the intention that their child will one day be an adult that has no idea how to shop, cook, clean, balance a checkbook, do laundry or handle a conflict. The intention is to be nice, helpful, and supportive, to create a life free of hard work and conflict.

But what have we actually done?

At work, we've prevented ourselves from getting a raise or a promotion. (By the way, men never do that.) We've also kept future leaders from learning and leading.

At home, we've created families that depend on us for everything, and robbed ourselves of precious time to enjoy experiences. We've kept our spouses and children from important lessons and experiences that will help them to be better functioning adults.

Ladies, this behavior is contagious. When you model for others that women should do all the work and not be compensated, that women don't need sick time or vacation time, that you don't mind doing it all and you are "fine", you're showing everyone around you that this behavior is acceptable and appropriate.

In my case, when I took over the cases of my co-workers, I taught them that if they feel tired, intimidated or overwhelmed, that Beth can handle it. I was admired for my enthusiasm, creativity, innovative problem solving and high energy level. I wasn't paid more, and they weren't paid less for doing less.

When I was completely depleted and full of resentment, I quit. The company lost a great employee, the clients got mediocre care and I showed everyone that social work is a field that burns you out.

If I could do it over again, I would certainly change the way I handled things. Instead of taking over, I might offer suggestions. Perhaps create a resource list that was shared with the entire agency, or multiple agencies. Maybe I could have created a forum where ideas for solving tough cases were shared and input gained from several sources. I could have made a point of leaving work on time, doing work at work, not at home, and enjoying earned vacation time. This would have modeled strong boundaries and a sensible but professional work ethic. I can't go back and change the choices that I made in the past but I can do my best to work smart and make sensible choices now.

Do you find yourself frequently solving other people's problems? Does your work day usually involve taking care of everyone else's issues before having the opportunity to address your own work? Do you have to stay late at work or come in early to have the opportunity to get your own work done? Have you created a situation at home or at work where you've trained other people to depend on you for everything? Don't panic, and don't beat yourself up. You created this situation with the best of intentions. Now you have the opportunity to make changes that will allow the people around you to step into their own leadership and adult roles. Let me give you some tips.

First, don't expect everyone to enthusiastically embrace your ideas for change. Some people would prefer that you keep doing their work and handling their issues. They may be very uncomfortable having to deal with things that they've never tackled before. Also, if you are a woman with high standards, they may fear that they cannot do things as well as you, so they might resist even trying. Be patient and be positive. Say something like this: "Sue, I understand that handling this case all by yourself seems intimidating. I've seen your work and I'm confident that you can handle this. I'll be right here if you get stuck, but I'm certain you won't. You're going to do great." Or this: "Son, I have great news. I'm going to be taking a vacation for the first time in 12 years. While I'm gone, you're going to need to cook for yourself. Let's practice preparing some meals together before I leave. What about a Sunday afternoon cooking lesson?"

Next, don't expect things to work out well immediately. You've spent years doing it all. It's going to take others a while to learn these tasks and even longer to master them. Remember, it took you a while to master them yourself. Resist the urge to take the tasks back. You might find yourself saying, "Never mind, I'll just do it. It takes me less time." Instead say, "Don't be frustrated. It took me a few months to learn to do that well."

Encourage people to solve issues on their own. It helps to have some statements prepared ahead of time, so that you can resist the urge to take over. Here are some of my favorites:

"I don't think I can help you with that right now, have you thought of asking John?"
"Yes, of course I can help you with that. I'm booked solid until after 4pm. Can we work on it then?"

"Of course I have time. I have 10 minutes before my next call. How can I help?"

"Hmm...that is a problem. What solutions have you tried?"

"What do you think would work?"

"Why don't you think of some solutions and let's meet again tomorrow morning. My first appointment is at 9am. Can you meet at 8:45am? I look forward to hearing what you come up with."

Notice how these examples set clear boundaries. Not only do they help you resist the urge to take over, they also send the clear message that the responsibility is theirs, your time is limited and you trust in their ability to do it without you.

Finally, I want to suggest that you guard your new time carefully. The "doing it all" habit has been with you for years. New projects will be tempting. Others will try and persuade you to slip back into your old habits. Remember to be intentional with your time. Rely on your ideal calendar and focus on your own work first. Trust me, you will really enjoy going home from work every night on time.

**New Habit
Number Eight:**

Hang Out With
Like-Minded People

Eleven
Find Like-Minded Friends

Do your friends get frustrated with you when you talk about your dreams, goals and desires? Do people often warn that you are becoming "too big for your britches" or ask, "Why do you always have to be different?" These are the types of questions and comments that I got from my friends for years. One day a professional colleague, Coach Monique said to me, "Beth, I think that you are trying to keep yourself small so that the people around you will feel comfortable." At that moment, I understood why people say "BAM".

Coach Monique was exactly right. It seemed like as long as I did everything and thought everything the same way as the people I was socializing with, everything was fine. Whenever I would get excited about starting a business or hosting an event, the people around me became uncomfortable. They often criticized and discouraged me. Everyone, that is, except for the women in my mastermind group. Those women were always delighted to hear my new ideas. They were impressed with my strategic thinking, my resourcefulness and creativity. They encouraged me to try out some of my ideas and take risks. When I was at my mastermind group, I felt like I fit in. The women that I met with each month also had high energy, clever ideas and were enthusiastic about their lives and businesses. Being with them made me happy. I felt supported and optimistic. In between these meetings, my enthusiasm would wane. I told myself that negativity was contagious and that I didn't have enough self-confidence to withstand critical comments. I noticed that other women were not as sensitive and didn't have the need for approval and acceptance that I was striving for. Still, I willed myself to tolerate criticism and strived to remain positive despite the drain on my energy levels. That one brief comment from Coach Monique changed everything. I finally realized that I didn't need to be more resilient, less sensitive or any stronger than I already was. I needed to find new friends. I was determined to fit in and be accepted by everyone, but the truth is that people prefer to be around like minds. You and I are no different. Seeking new friends and social situations was somewhat awkward for me. I make new friends very easily but I felt guilty about leaving old friends behind. For some reason, I felt obligated to keep them comfortable and not offend them. If you are like me, perhaps you can relate. I had a very important lesson to learn:

Not all friendships are meant to last a lifetime.

Some friends come into our lives for a very short time. Very few are lifelong relationships. I wasted a lot of time, energy and emotions trying to force these friendships into lifelong commitments.

Are you feeling drained by the people you spend your time with? While you might choose to tolerate difficult people in your family or at your workplace, you can and should choose the friends that you associate with. Think about your life right now and the people in it.

- Do they make you laugh?
- Do they encourage your ideas?
- Do they nurture you during tough times?
- Does thinking of them lift your spirits?

If the answer to these questions is not yes or if you're spending most of your free time alone, then let's strive for something new. Where can you locate new friends that share your ideas and passions?

For me, it began with my mastermind group. Look for groups of people that share the same interests as you. I've met some soul-mates at business conferences, networking events and fundraisers. If your passion is business growth, try that.

Do you need some new social friends? Join a book club. If you want to make a difference with a non-profit organization, call one and volunteer. Attend fundraisers to get out and meet people who also want to make a difference. Visit your local Rotary Club or check out GiveWell.org to find charities that make deep impacts. Do you feel strongly that our country needs a change in leadership? Don't just vote, get involved with your political party. Another interest of mine is social justice. To learn more about that topic, look for Unitarian Universalist churches in your area. If you want to write a book, look for writers groups. The possibilities are endless!

Friends are like vegetables, they are all good! You don't need to stop speaking to your friends and family, simply add some variety to your salad. When you begin spending time with like-minded people, I promise you'll feel more vital.

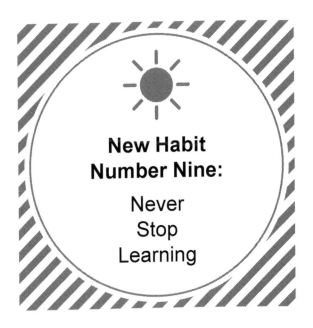

**New Habit
Number Nine:**

Never
Stop
Learning

Twelve
Be a Life-Long Learner

One of my favorite people in the universe is Dr. Wayne Dyer. I've read most of his books several times, listened to his audio recordings and watched him on public television. When I feel stuck, I go to YouTube and look for a Dr. Wayne video to inspire me. Although he died in 2015, people continue to benefit from his teachings every day because we can access his works with modern media.

Early in his career, Dr. Wayne spoke at churches in Michigan driving in his station wagon across the state with his family and boxes of books in the back. Later, he taught conferences for groups around the world. At that time, the only way to benefit from his teachings was by purchasing his book or attending an event in person. Limited numbers of people were able to access this information. Colleges and Universities were once available only to a select few, and still are in many countries in the world. Today education comes in many more forms than traditional university learning.

I am a life-long learner, an avid reader, listener and viewer of knowledge and information. When we weren't listening to books on tape in the car, my boys heard motivational and training programs while in their car seats. Today I regularly attend business conferences, read books and publications every day and attend courses by web-cast each week.

At this point in my career, I'm a sought - after expert, and it is not because of a college degree or certificate (I have neither). I have acquired knowledge that makes me invaluable to my clients and inspirational to my audiences.

What would you like to learn more about? Do you want to learn a new language, take up a musical instrument, run for political office, program your computer, renovate your home, start an online business, get a raise or promotion? In today's world you can do anything. The knowledge is literally at your fingertips.

Women often complain to me, "But Beth, I have no time to take a class". That may be true. But you can choose to read a book each night instead of watching TV, or listen to a workshop instead of the news while you're driving. Instead of seeing limitations, look for possibilities, they are everywhere.

New Habit Number Ten:

Treat Yourself Well Everyday

Thirteen
Treat Yourself Well

Just after Christmas this year, I was shopping at Bed Bath and Beyond. Mom and Dad had given me a $100 gift certificate to treat myself. My cart was filling fast, and it looked like I was going to have to add some of my own money at checkout. As I reviewed the items in my cart I was gleefully checking off my shopping list:

- ☑ Towels for Brian
- ☑ Sheets for Kevin
- ☑ Shower gift for February
- ☑ Wedding gift for April
- ☑ Cleaning supplies
- ☑ Candles for last minute gifts

I was pleased with myself. Then I remembered my mom stressing to me, "Beth, get something for yourself." Hmmm…. nothing in the cart was for me. I am so accustomed to taking care of others that it never occurred to me to shop just for myself. "What do I even want?", I asked myself. I started to feel uncomfortable at the idea of spending money to pamper myself. Brian didn't need any towels and Kevin didn't need any sheets. My kitchen and bathroom closets are well-stocked with cleaning supplies. I can get wedding gifts with my own money. I kept thinking, "What do I really really want?" I wandered a little, feeling uneasy. A thought popped into my mind. "Egyptian sheets!"

I smiled. Whenever I visit my favorite spa in the world, ESSpa, for a facial or massage, I adore snuggling into their amazing soft sheets. "That's exactly what I want!" I turned my cart and a salesperson was right there. "Can I help you with anything?" she said in a friendly tone. (One of the many things I like about Bed Bath and Beyond is their friendly staff.) "Yes, please," I replied. "Can you put back all these things?" I said, as I rushed back to the sheet section of the store. I spent the next thirty minutes feeling and sniffing Egyptian Cotton. I was delighted to come to the register with my $100 gift card and two sets of new sheets. Yes, I did have to add money to pay the bill, and yes I adore snuggling into those sheets each night. Well-deserved luxury.

Treat yourself well everyday by doing things that feed your soul.

Pampering yourself is what I want you to do every day. This doesn't just mean taking an occasional trip to the spa. Treat yourself well everyday by doing things that feed your soul. Here are some of my favorites:

- Sleeping in
- Reading
- Walks in nature
- Beautiful music
- Visiting people I love
- Visit to ESSpa
- Girls night in with friends
- Bubble baths

- Work in my garden

Some of my friends enjoy yoga, swimming, hiking, long walks, bike riding, knitting and journaling. You might enjoy painting, drawing, playing music, singing, or shopping for new sheets. Think about what makes your soul happy and do that. But definitely buy nice sheets, friends. You deserve them.

Fourteen
Beth's Favorite Time-Saving Tips

It seems like I'm always giving and being asked for my tips. Over the years I've come up with lots and lots of time-saving strategies. Add these to your own favorites.

At Home

Give each person a clothes basket or hamper for their dirty clothes. Instead of waiting until everything is dirty, assign each person their own laundry day.

Keep clothes hangers on your clothes line or next to the dryer. This way you'll be able to immediately hang your good clothes and avoid the need to iron.

Keep a bin, box or bag in the laundry room for your Goodwill donations. As your family grows out of clothing, you can fold them and put them into the Goodwill box right out of the dryer.

Keep your crafty things in clear bins. For those of you who knit, scrapbook, stamp, or do other crafts, these tiny items can get lost all over the house. I enjoy scrapbooking. I have several nice acrylic, wood, and plastic boxes to keep all of these supplies nicely organized and all in one place.

Have a tote bag for each activity so that you can keep items organized and off of the floor. We used to have a tote bag for library books. Whenever you're done with a book, it goes into the bag so it's ready to go to the library. You can have a bag for dry cleaning, sports, church activities, crafts, clubs and organizations. This keeps you streamlined and organized and you're not searching for things when it's time to walk out the door.

Have a plastic binder in the kitchen with your family's favorite recipes. I used to keep a document on my computer, but printing out the recipes is better. We put the recipes in page protectors to keep them safe from spills. You can sort these recipes by Breakfast, Lunch, Dinner, Snacks, Smoothies, etc., as they do in cookbooks. A fun extra step is to assign each family a color and print their favorite recipes on colored paper. That way you can take turns cooking one another's favorite dishes.

Print up grocery lists and keep them in a binder or on the refrigerator. You can create your own list with your common items, or make a blank one. As soon as you run out of something, or whenever you plan to cook a recipe, write the item on the list. Yes, you can keep digital lists, but then your family is not participating. For very nice printables, visit Abby Lawson's blog at JustAGirlAndHerBlog.com.

Declutter every day. Paper and other items tend to gather on countertops and tables. Spend a few minutes each day tackling clutter so it does not get out of control. When putting things away, instead of saying "Where should I put this?", ask yourself, "Where will I find this?" This is a tip that I learned from Patty Kreamer's book, **The Power of Simplicity**, and I use it every day.

Have a special place to keep your bills and invoices.
Instead of leaving your bills and correspondence out on your table, have a special box or area where bills are placed. Many of my accounts are on autopay, and most are paid by electronic banking now, but I still get a lot of paper statements. My bill box is a very pretty floral box that I bought at Marshalls. It's the right size to fit inside the top of my buffet drawer, and it's pretty enough that I feel good when I open my bills.

Open your mail over the recycle bin. Instead of letting your mail pile up, open everything right over the recycle or trash bin. The items that are not needed go into the recycle bin. Other items can go on your bulletin board, into your "to do" folder or in the bill box.

To keep your furnace and other household appliances running smoothly, put maintenance of these items into your family calendar. If you use an electronic calendar, have them automatically repeat annually or as needed. If you use a paper calendar do this every December or January. Some of the items on my appliance calendar are:

- Change furnace filter
- Replace smoke detector batteries
- Cover A/C unit for the winter
- Uncover A/C for the summer
- Clean gutters
- Check dryer vent
- Clean refrigerator coils
- Treat drains with root killer (spring and fall)

In The Car

My car used to be a MESS, and it often smelled like soccer socks. My family used to joke about it and one day my niece, Mia, about 3 years old at the time said, "Aunt Beth, your car is disgusting." I don't enjoy a messy car or house. I like to be in neat and comfy surroundings. The problem with my car was that I was always on the run, never leaving time between commitments to even empty the car. Once at a baseball game someone needed water, bandages and ibuprofen. I had all three of these items in the back seat of my car. About this time I read a book called **FlyLady** by Marla Cilley. (view her blog at FlyLady.net) Marla taught me to clean out my car once a week. I did this every Wednesday when I dropped the boys off at Christian Boy's Club. I had about 90 minutes after dropping them off and that was just enough to do weekly grocery shopping and stop by the car wash. I kept a few empty bins in the trunk so I could easily sort trash, library books, food, clothing, school projects and sports equipment. I'd put these sorted items in the trunk and vacuum the carpeting and seats. Kevin would never notice but Brian would always say, "Wow, Mom, you've been busy."

Today I keep the car neat by making it a point to empty the trash and clutter every time I fill up with gas. Teach your children to do this with you. Whenever you pull into the gas station, have them look around and gather up any trash. Clothes and sports equipment can be sorted and organized during the few minutes that it takes to fill the tank. This is an important life skill that they will carry into adulthood.

Keep up with car maintenance with calendar reminders. If you use an electronic calendar, add the dates needed for car inspection, oil changes, filter changes battery check-ups with the "auto-repeat" function, or enter these in your written planner each January.

Garage

I have to give Paul full credit for keeping my garage organized. He hates a messy garage. Every spring and fall he takes everything out of the garage, sweeps the floor and hoses it down. He organizes the gardening equipment and tools, repairs or throws out what is broken and puts everything back on a hook or shelf. We have large bins that we keep potting soil, fertilizer and salt in so that the bags are not scattered everywhere. A clean garage has never been top priority for me, but driving in and out of one sure is nice.

In The Community

At the grocery store, park on the side of the building. When Kevin was young, he had a tendency to dash. This made crossing traffic to get inside the grocery store very stressful. Some of you are at the grocery store alone, some with young children and some with aging family members. No matter what your situation, parking on the side of the building is safer and usually less crowded.

When you are parking at a mall or large lot, pause when you get out of your car. Look up at the store and line your car up with a landmark. If you're parking at Target, notice that your car is in the same row as the letter G. Teach your children to do this with you. "Help Mom remember where the car is parked. What letter is that?" The kids are learning their letters and you are teaching them life management skills at the same time. This is a good exercise for older adults too. It helps to avoid panic when you come out of the store.

When entering a parking garage, go directly to the top or bottom floor. Driving through a parking garage while looking for an open space is so stressful. Make it easy on yourself by driving right to the top floor, or to the bottom floor if the garage is underground. Most of the time the entire floor is open so you can park near the elevator for added safety. Once you've parked your car, put the parking ticket into your wallet next to your cash, so you will not have to search for it later. To remember where you parked, write down the floor and location on your parking ticket, or take a photo of the floor designation with your cell phone.

Travel

Traveling should be fun, not stressful. To keep myself prepared, I have some travel routines that I rely one. I always make sure that my luggage is in good repair before I put it away after each trip. I also have a duplicate set of all of my toiletries and cosmetics that I keep with my suitcase. Whenever I find a lipstick or blush color that I love, I order two. One goes in my makeup drawer at home and the other goes in my travel bag. When it's about time to re-order mascara or eyeliner, I keep the new one at home and the used one goes into the travel bag. I have duplicate hair styling and skin care products, so packing for travel is simple. I use good quality cosmetic and travel bags that I purchased from Baggalini. They travel well and don't tear or break open. Invest in good quality, sturdy luggage.

Be flexible when traveling and allow for delays. If I have to speak at a conference out of town, I make sure that my flight arrives more than 24 hours before my presentation. No matter where you're going, you don't want to be stressed when you arrive because of airport delays.

I keep a tote-bag with reading materials just for travel. As you know, I'm an avid reader. I don't like to read on devices, so I'll often print out e-books to read while I'm on the road. Sometimes I don't have time to read my Oprah or Success Magazines so I keep them in my travel tote as well. Whenever I'm done, I leave them in the travel lounge for someone else to enjoy.

Personal

Keep your closets and drawers organized so that you feel good when you are looking at your clothes and selecting what to wear. If there are clothing items that don't flatter you or that you don't look and feel good in, donate them. There is a woman out there who will be blessed by your gift. Sort your clothes in a way that makes sense to you. I have my closet organized from left to right tanks, short sleeves, long sleeves, jackets, sweaters pants, skirts, dresses. Purses are hung on hooks at the back of the closet and shoes are stacked on floor shelves. My shoes are organized left to right, sandals, casual shoes, dress shoes, boots. I have a large zippered storage bag that I use for seasonal item storage. If your clothing drawers are over-full then you probably have too many clothes. Sort one drawer at a time and discard anything old, stained, torn or ugly. Don't donate items that you would not wear. Make a separate pile for clothes to donate and then neatly fold and return the remaining items to your drawer. Getting dressed in the morning should not be stressful!

If you are a book lover like me, then you probably have lots and lots of books. Some women shop for clothes, makeup and jewelry, I spend my dollars at Barnes and Noble.

At one time I had to make a rule that if we brought any new books into the house then the same number of books had to be released. You can sell old books, but I prefer to donate quality books to schools, shelters or reading programs for the incarcerated.

Every few months, dump out and organize your makeup and cosmetic bags. I have a cosmetic drawer and two travel cosmetic bags. When you have that much space, I tend to collect items. My hard and fast rule is that if it doesn't work, I don't keep it. To save money and time, I tend to be very loyal to cosmetics that work for me. I don't like spending money on mascara and then having to throw it away because it smudges under my eyes. The skin care system that I use is Arbonne. This company offers botanical products that are safe, gentle and don't irritate my skin. (shop here: franmel.myarbonne.com) My cosmetics come from Mary Kay or Melaleuca. All three of these companies let me return products that don't work and all of them deliver to my door. I like to keep my cosmetic containers neat and clean, so whenever I organize my cosmetics I use a cloth with hot soapy water to wipe everything, including the brushes and the inside of the drawer. Use a gentle soap that won't damage your brushes. Keep your makeup area dust free and clean your mirror every week. Never look at yourself in a dirty mirror!

Keep your jewelry organized and repaired. I spent one Saturday afternoon many years ago organizing my jewelry. It doesn't make sense to spend precious minutes in the morning searching for an earring. I purchased a wall-mount jewelry organizer for my necklaces and this is hung next to my dresser mirror. (Yes, I bought it at Bed Bath and Beyond!) I also purchased a ring organizer, a bracelet rack and a velvet-lined tray with lots of little boxes for my earrings and charms. I put these items in the top drawer of my dresser. Some of my jewelry tarnishes in velvet, so later I bought a small ceramic container for my finer jewelry, and this fits right next to my earring box. Whenever I remove my jewelry, I spend a few seconds putting it on a hook or in the jewelry drawer. This makes getting ready in the morning or packing for a trip effortless. If your jewelry is broken or your watch needs a new battery do not put it away. If it can be repaired, put it in a bag and put the bag in your purse to take to the repair shop, if not, discard or have it melted depending on the quality of the jewelry. Don't ever donate broken jewelry because you're burdening the non-profit with the time and cost of discarding it. If you find that you have too much jewelry, then donate the pieces that you don't love to an organization that helps women in transition, or give it to a girl who enjoys playing dress up. (Don't give small jewelry to children under 3, or those who may choke)

Keep your finances organized. Whenever we are busy, financial things get overlooked. Be smart about your money and avoid service fees or excess charges by keeping your financial records organized. No matter how much or how little money you have saved, you should be working with a financial advisor. Meet with your financial advisor twice a year to be sure that your savings and investments are ideal. Your financial advisor may also help you to identify places where you're overspending and strategies to help you save more. My advisor is Lisa Krall, get a free financial checkup with her here: ParkAveWealth.com.

Keep your home a sanctuary. Your home is where you eat, sleep relax and refresh yourself. You should not feel stressed, worried or overwhelmed when you walk into your door. If it's become cluttered and chaotic, block time in your calendar to regain control and block time every week for cleaning and maintenance. I've learned that it's better to spend fifteen minutes a day keeping things organized and clean than spending your entire weekend or holiday cleaning and exhausting yourself. Small efforts every day pay off. If you need help, call my friend Jill Yesko who is a professional organizer and works with clients anywhere in the world. Find her at DiscoverOrganizing.com.

Beautify your landscape. When you are pulling into your driveway or walking to your door, I want you to feel happy to be home. Landscaping does not have to be complicated, a few pretty flowers or well-placed planters make you happy to be home. My flower boxes make me feel joyful. I enjoy shopping for annual blossoms every May and carefully choose the blooms that I'll see right outside my door. It's the first thing I see when I leave the house and the last thing I see before I come in the door. Little things like this make a difference in your attitude. Be sure that the outside of your home is tidy, too. Sweep up your porch, clean doors and light fixtures, power-wash awnings, paint or re-stain your deck or patio area. Always have a beautiful wreath on your door and a nice welcome mat, I want you to feel happy every time you come home.

Calendarize everything you want to do. I attended a workshop by author Elissa Ashwood last year. Her book is **Calendaring Happiness**. She taught me to schedule the things that are important to me so I'd be sure to get them done. As I was listening to her speak about her program (check out CalendaringHappiness.com) I imagined the dusty bags in my dining room with donations for some charities that I support. I had some books for a charter school in one bag, used ink cartridges for another school in a different bag, and used video games in yet another bag for a children's shelter. My intention was to deliver these donations personally, but I never seemed to have the time. That evening while I was listening to Elissa speak, I pulled up my online calendar and selected dates to visit each organization. Simple as that.

Keep your purse clean and organized. This is another great strategy that I learned from FlyLady.net. Clean out your purse every Friday. Sort your receipts and either discard them or file for bookkeeping. Organize your credit and debit cards, straighten out your cash, put your change into the zipper pouch and throw away all the tissues and scraps of paper. Shake out the purse over the trash can to get rid of any crumbs that have found their way there. Put your lipstick, powder, business cards, glasses, etc. back into the right compartments, and zip it up. This should take you less than 5 minutes each week. When your purse is a mess you feel scattered. Keep it organized and you'll feel more calm and confident.

Have lots of purses? Keep purse-switching stress free. In each purse I keep a ready supply of business cards, tissues, lip balm and, and anti-bacterial wipes. Whenever I switch purses I only need to grab my wallet, my cell phone and my essential oil bag. When I'm done using a purse, I clean it out and replenish before hanging it back on it's hook.

Stretch and move every day. For many years I sat at my desk writing and talking on the phone, taking very few breaks. At the end of the day I'd feel stiff and sore. Our bodies were not designed to sit in chairs all day long. Stretching is a good way to keep yourself flexible and avoid stiffness. If you don't exercise much, you'll want to start slow, and work on your balance. Balance is very important as we age. It's good for posture, helps you stay coordinated and can prevent you from falling. To improve your balance, practice standing on one leg every day. Try to do this for twenty seconds on each leg without holding on to the wall. This is a great exercise to do with the entire family. If you're having trouble sleeping at night, chances are you may not be moving enough. If you don't want to take a thirty minute walk every day, try and take 3 ten minute walks.

Quiet your mind frequently. As I mentioned in chapter nine, quieting your brain is good for you. I recently read that meditation and deep breathing can have a positive effect on high blood pressure, anxiety, headaches and other common issues that are caused by stress. Some good resources to try are calm.com, meditationoasis.com and mindful.org.

My most important tip to you is this: **Yes you CAN do it all**, you just can't do it all at the same time. Remember that every day. Don't beat yourself up, don't compare yourself to other women, stop "shoulding" yourself. You are exactly who you are meant to be right now. Embrace that. Focus on your gifts. Listen to your soul. Take life one day at a time, and remember that most of us are doing the best we can. Forgive yourself. Other women are watching. When you stop being frantic, you'll give them permission to do the same.

Meet the Author

Beth Caldwell is a professional speaker, WebTV host and influencer. Her mission is to inspire and motivate women to be their best selves.

She is a columnist for the *Pittsburgh Business Times* newspaper and *Smart Business* magazine, but is best known as the founder of Pittsburgh Professional Women and Leadership Academy for Women. **From Frantic to Focused** is her fourth book.

Recognized by Pittsburgh Magazine as an influential and innovative leader, Beth was named a "40 Under 40" winner the day before her 40th birthday. She's also been recognized with the Pennsylvania Woman of Courage Award. Beth teaches workshops on leadership, business, and inspiration to audiences worldwide for the Steve Harvey Success Institute. She is the mom of two college age sons and the mischievous adolescent JJ Kitty.

Watch her WebTV channel online here:
pittsburghbiztvshows.com

Connect on social media here:
facebook.com/InspiredbyBethCaldwell
pinterest.com/bethacaldwell
twitter.com/beth_a_caldwell
linkedin.com/in/bethcaldwell

To hire Beth to speak for your conference or organization, call (412) 202-6983 or email beth@beth-caldwell.com.

Made in the USA
Middletown, DE
03 June 2017